EXODUS

EXO⬡

Adapted from the Bible by
MIRIAM CHAIKIN
Illustrated by
CHARLES MIKOLAYCAK

DUS

יציאת מצרים

Holiday House/New York

Library of Congress Cataloging-in-Publication Data

Chaikin, Miriam.
Exodus.

SUMMARY: Retells the Biblical story of Moses leading
his enslaved people out of Egypt.
1. Exodus, The—Juvenile literature. [1. Moses
(Biblical leader)   2. Exodus, The.   3. Bible stories—
O.T.]   I. Mikolaycak, Charles, ill.   II. Title.
BS680.E9C48   1987   222′.1209505   85-27361
ISBN 0-8234-0607-5

יְצִיאַת מִצְרִים

Exodus, the second book of the Bible, was originally known by its Hebrew name, *Sefer Yitziat Mitzraim, The Book of Going Out of Egypt*. In about 250 B.C., the Bible was translated into Greek. The Greek Bible was called *Septuagint*, which means seventy, for the number of Hebrew scholars (actually seventy-two) who made the translation. The second book was translated as *Exodos*, a Greek word meaning "Road Out."

The Latin spelling, *Exodus*, occurred in the fourth century A.D., when St. Jerome prepared the Vulgate, a Latin translation of the Bible. The Latin name remained in all subsequent English translations.

The author consulted the *King James Version of the Bible*, the *Revised Standard Version*, the *Bible of the Jewish Publication Society*, *The New American Bible*, and other English translations in preparing the text for this book.

There arose in Egypt a new king who said to his people, "The Israelites are too many and too mighty. Let us deal wisely with them, lest they multiply and it comes to pass when we go to war that they join our enemies."

The Egyptians enslaved the Israelites and set them to work in the sun making bricks. But the pharaoh was not satisfied. "Let every son that is born of the Israelites be killed," he said.

Among the Israelites were Yochebed and Amram, whose children were Aaron and Miriam. And after the pharaoh's decree another child, a boy, was born to them, and they were afraid for his life. Yochebed made an ark of bulrushes in which to hide the boy. She lined the ark with pitch and set it on the river, where the pharaoh's daughter went to bathe. And Yochebed's own daughter, Miriam, hid behind the bulrushes to watch.

When the pharaoh's daughter came to the river and saw the boy, she loved him and said, "This is one of the Hebrews' children." Miriam hurried to the princess and said, "Shall I call a Hebrew nursing woman to nurse the child for you?" And the princess said, "Go."

Thus it was that Yochebed, the boy's own mother, came to nurse him, and that the princess adopted him, and gave him the name Moses, saying, "Because I drew him out of the water."

Now it came to pass, when Moses was grown, that he was saddened to see his people toiling from sunup to sundown. And when he came upon an Egyptian overseer smiting a Hebrew, he became enraged and slew the Egyptian. Because the pharaoh was angry, Moses fled to Midian, where he married Zipporah, the daughter of Jethro, the priest.

Moses tended Jethro's flocks. And one day when he led them out toward Mount Horeb, which is Sinai, he saw an angel of flame appear out of a bush that burned with fire but was not consumed. Out of its midst the voice of God called, "Moses, Moses," and with a quaking heart, Moses answered, "Here am I."

"I am the God of your ancestors," God said. "The Israelites suffer greatly in Egypt, I have heard their cries. Go to them and say the Lord God of their fathers, Abraham, Isaac and Jacob, has appeared to you. Tell the pharaoh to let them go, and take them to Canaan, a land flowing with milk and honey, which I have promised their ancestors to give them."

"Who am I, that I should speak to the pharaoh?" Moses asked. "And who am I that the Israelites should obey me?"

"What is that in your hand?" God asked.

"A rod," Moses answered.

"Cast it on the ground," God said.

Moses did so, and the rod became a serpent, and Moses recoiled from it.

God told Moses to take it by the tail, and when Moses did so, the serpent became a rod again.

"Go, speak to the pharaoh," God said. "I will give you signs and wonders to perform. Let him know that I am the Lord."

"Oh, Lord," Moses said, "I am slow of tongue and speak poorly."

"Take your brother Aaron to speak for you," God said. "I will put words in your mouth, and you will put them in his. And take the rod you hold."

Moses parted with his father-in-law. He set his wife and sons upon an ass, and journeyed out with his rod, and met Aaron in the wilderness on the way, and they went to Egypt.

There they came before the pharaoh, and the words that God spoke to Moses, Moses spoke to Aaron, and Aaron repeated. "Thus says the Lord, my God," Moses said to the pharaoh. "*Let my people go, that they may worship me in the wilderness.*"

"Who is your God that I should listen to him?" the pharaoh said. To his overseers, he said, "If the Israelites have time to go to the wilderness to worship, then they are too idle. Hold back the straw they need to make bricks. Let them gather their own straw, yet turn out the same number of bricks each day."

The Israelites could not search for straw and also turn out the same number of bricks, so the overseers beat them.

Moses complained to God, saying, "Why have you sent me? The pharaoh has grown more evil. Nor have you saved the Israelites."

"Now you will see what I will do to the pharaoh," God said. God remained speaking to Moses for some time, telling him what to do. And as Moses was commanded, so he and Aaron did.

The pharaoh taunted them, saying, "Show me a miracle." Whereupon Moses told Aaron to cast his rod before the pharaoh, and when Aaron did, the rod became a serpent. The pharaoh called upon his magicians to do the same with their rods, and they also made serpents. Aaron performed another wonder, and his rod swallowed the other rods, but the pharaoh remained hardhearted and would not let the Israelites go.

In the morning, Moses and Aaron went to the river bank to see the pharaoh. Moses repeated God's words, saying, "Let my people go, that they may worship me in the wilderness." To show the power of God, Aaron smote the river with his rod and the water turned to blood. When the pharaoh's magicians did the same with their magic, the pharaoh did not answer, but only turned and went inside.

Again and again Moses and Aaron went before the pharaoh speaking God's words, and warning what affliction God would send if he refused to listen. But the pharaoh would not heed the warning and bend to God's will.

Aaron stretched out his hand over the waters, and frogs leapt out and covered the land. The palace magicians, with their magic, also brought forth frogs. The pharaoh sent for Moses and Aaron and said, "Ask your God to take the frogs from the land and I will let your people go." But when God returned the frogs to the waters, the pharaoh became hardhearted and did not let the Israelites go.

God then sent lice, and lice crawled upon people and upon beasts. The palace magicians also tried to bring forth lice, but could not, and they said to the pharaoh, "This is the finger of God." And they asked the pharaoh to let the Israelites go. But the pharaoh would not listen.

God sent swarms of flies to Egypt, but not to Goshen, where the Israelites lived, for Goshen was spared. The flies brought ruin to the land of the Egyptians, and the pharaoh sent for Moses and Aaron and told them the Israelites could sacrifice to God, but in the land of Egypt, not in the wilderness.

"We cannot sacrifice here," Moses said, "for the animals we sacrifice are holy to the Egyptians, and will they not stone us for it?"

The pharaoh said he would allow the Israelites to serve God in the wilderness if God removed the swarms of flies. But the pharaoh did not keep his word, for when the flies were gone, he again refused to let the Israelites go.

A cattle disease then destroyed the cattle, large and small, of the Egyptians. Then boils afflicted their flesh and the flesh of their beasts. Then a hailstorm, followed by swarms of locusts, destroyed their crops and their herbs and trees. The Egyptians themselves begged the pharaoh to let the Israelites go worship, but his heart remained hard.

God sent a ninth plague to afflict the Egyptians, and a great and heavy darkness lay over the land. "Take the Israelites, and go worship your God," the pharaoh said to Moses and Aaron. "But leave your flocks and herds behind."

"The Israelites need their animals, to make sacrifices to the Lord," Moses said. Whereupon the pharaoh banished Moses from his sight forever.

The pharaoh was warned by God about a tenth plague but he would not listen. So God sent yet one more plague, the slaying of the firstborn. And at midnight, the angel of death went over the land. He passed over the houses of the Hebrews. But he touched the houses of the Egyptians and their firstborn sons died, also the firstborn of their cattle. And the son of the pharaoh also died. A great cry went up in the land, the like of which was never heard before and will never be heard again.

At last, the pharaoh sent for Moses and Aaron in the night and said, "Depart, you and the Israelites, and go serve the Lord, as you have said."

In haste, the Israelites took their flocks and herds and the dough they had been leavening. They put their kneading troughs upon their shoulders, and they followed Moses and Aaron out of Egypt.

"Remember this day always," Moses said to them. "For your houses were passed over, and your firstborn were spared, and the Lord brought you out of Egypt, where you were slaves." And in the wilderness, in the month of Abib, the people celebrated the Passover. They baked unleavened cakes of the dough. And they slaughtered and roasted lambs, which they ate, and gave thanks to the Lord.

The heart of the pharaoh soured toward what he had done. And his advisors also cried over the loss of slaves. "Why have we let the Israelites go from serving us?" they cried. The pharaoh prepared chariots and men, and went out after the Israelites, to bring them back.

The Israelites were at the sea, and when they saw the Egyptians pursuing them, they were angry and afraid. "Were there no graves in Egypt, that you had to take us to the wilderness to die?" they said to Moses.

Moses told them the Lord would save them. And he took up his rod, at God's command, and stretched it over the sea, and a strong wind came from the east and divided the waters in two. And the Israelites walked between the waters to the other side.

And when the Egyptians came after them, Moses again lifted his rod, and the waters came rushing together, drowning the Egyptians and their horses.

"*God is my strength and song, He is my salvation,*" Moses sang joyously. And Miriam, his sister, took up her tambourine and sang her own song: "*Sing to God, for He is highly exalted, the horse and his rider has He thrown into the sea.*"

The Israelites wandered on, following the pillar of cloud God had sent to lead them during the day, and the pillar of fire that led them at night. They grew tired and hungry, and began to murmur against Moses. "We had bread enough in Egypt, and you have brought us into the wilderness to kill us with hunger," they said to him.

God heard their murmuring and said to them, through the mouth of Moses, "You shall have flesh to eat in the evening and bread in the morning." And lo, in the evening, quails covered the wilderness and in the morning, manna, a white seed like coriander, whose taste was like wafers with honey.

In Rephidim, where the Israelites next encamped, they began to murmur again, because there was no water. "Have you taken us out of Egypt to kill us and our children and our cattle with thirst?" they said to Moses.

And Moses cried unto God, saying, "What shall I do with this people? They are almost ready to stone me."

God told Moses to take his rod and strike the rock at Horeb and Moses did so, and lo, water came forth, and the people had water to drink.

The Israelites then pitched their tents in the Sinai wilderness, near the mount. And God gave Moses words to say to the people, and Moses repeated them, saying, "You have seen what I have done for you. If you listen to my voice and keep my laws you shall be a special treasure to me, for all the earth is mine. And you shall be unto me a kingdom of priests, and a holy nation."

The people answered with one voice, "All that the Lord has spoken we will do."

Then God said to Moses, "In three days I will come in a thick cloud." Moses told this to the people, and they washed and changed their garments. And the third morning, Moses led them out to meet God. The mount before them was alive with thunders and lightnings, and a thick cloud, and blasts from a ram's horn. The people trembled as they stood at the foot of the mount, for the mount, which was covered with smoke, quaked, and the Lord descended in fire.

God spoke to the people through the mouth of Moses, saying, "I am the Lord your God who brought you out of Egypt to be your God. You shall have no other gods before me.. You shall not bow down to graven images, or take my name in vain. Remember the Sabbath, to keep it holy. Honor your father and mother. You shall not murder, commit adultery, or steal. You shall not bear false witness, nor covet your neighbor's possessions."

Moses repeated also other laws of right conduct which God had given him to repeat and the people answered, "All that the Lord has spoken, we will do, and we will listen."

Then on an altar of twelve stones, one stone for each tribe, which Moses had built, the people sacrificed oxen to the Lord.

"Come up to me," God said to Moses, "you and Aaron, and his two sons, and the seventy elders. Let them worship me from afar, but you come near. I will give you laws and commandments to teach the people."

Moses told the Israelites to hearken to Aaron. And he took Joshua, his minister, to accompany him to the mount. Joshua waited below, and Moses went up alone, into the midst of a cloud. And God spoke to him and gave him laws of worship, and told him to build a tabernacle, and to anoint Aaron and his descendants as priests. "Tell the people to keep the Sabbath, for it is a sign between me and the Israelites forever," God said. "For in six days I made heaven and earth, and on the seventh day I rested."

Moses went down the mount with laws for the people, and with two tables of stone, written with the finger of God. Noises came from the camp as he walked with Joshua. "It is not the noise of trouble, as of war, but of singing," Joshua said.

In the camp, the people were dancing around a golden calf. Moses had been gone forty days, and they feared he would not return. They had bothered Aaron to make a new god for them to worship. And Aaron had melted their rings and earrings and made the golden calf. And now they danced before the fire, worshiping the golden figure.

"You have sinned a very great sin," Moses cried in anger. And he cast down the tables, and broke them, and he threw the golden calf into the fire, and those who had danced before the calf he ordered slain.

When his anger had cooled, he returned to the mount to ask God to forgive the people.

"Depart," God said, "and take the people to the land which I promised Abraham, Isaac and Jacob to give to their seed."

God gave Moses rules for the people to obey when they reached Canaan, telling them to drive out the Canaanites and to destroy the idols that they worshiped, and to worship only God. And God commanded the people to keep the Passover, and the other festivals. And on two tables of stone, like the first two, Moses wrote the ten commandments. And when he went down from the mount, his face was radiant with the glory of God, and Aaron and the elders and all the people saw it.

Moses repeated to the people God's words, and told them God had asked them to build a tabernacle to God so that He might dwell among them.

The hearts of the people were stirred by love. They melted their rings and bracelets and earrings and made gold and silver for the tabernacle. Skilled workers made boards of acacia wood and skilled weavers wove curtains of blue and purple and scarlet. They made an ark of acacia wood overlaid with gold to hold the two tables of stone and two cherubim of gold to stand on either side of the ark. And they made two altars, one for burning sweet spices and the other for offering sacrifices to God.

And for Aaron, whom Moses had anointed high priest, they made a breastplate with twelve gems, a separate stone for each tribe, set in gold. They also made an ephod, and other priestly garments, and a crown of gold with a plate engraved with the words, *Holy to the Lord.*

All that God commanded, Moses told the people, and all that Moses said, the people did. When the work was completed, Moses set each thing in its place. And a cloud came over the Tabernacle, and the glory of the Lord filled it, and the people worshiped God.

When the cloud departed, the people took down their tents. Helper priests took down the Tabernacle and took up the ark. And they followed the pillar of cloud out of the camp, the Israelites marching behind them, and as God had commanded, they journeyed on to the Promised Land.

5747
CM·86

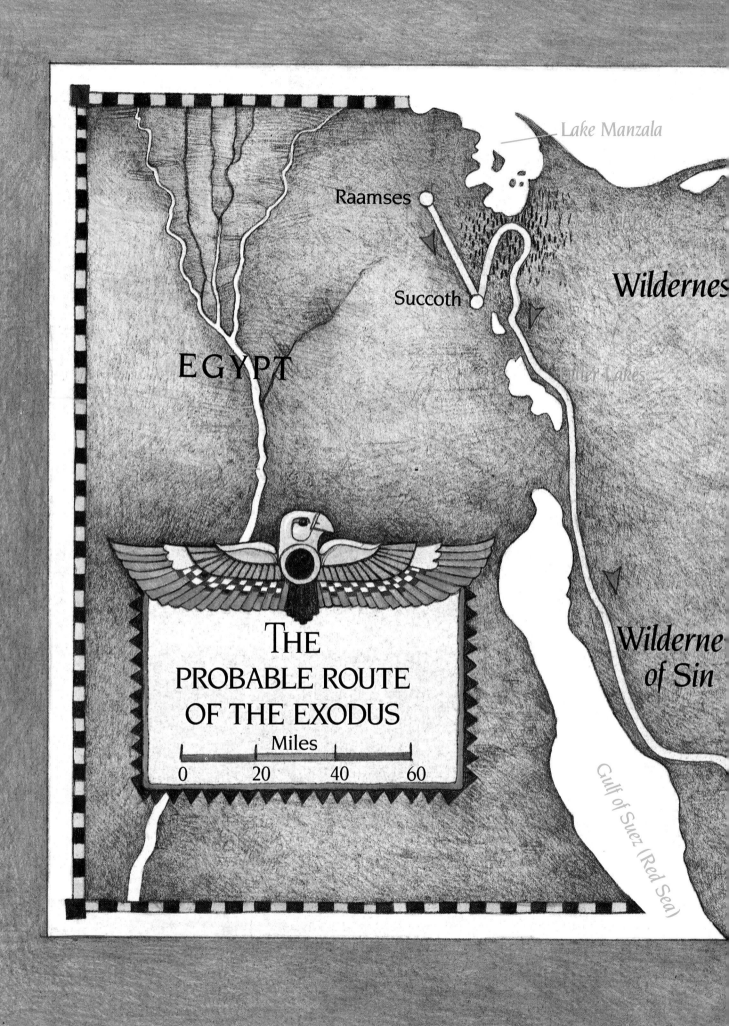

Lake Manzala

Raamses

Succoth

Wilderness

EGYPT

THE
PROBABLE ROUTE
OF THE EXODUS

Miles

0   20   40   60

Wilderness
of Sin

Gulf of Suez (Red Sea)

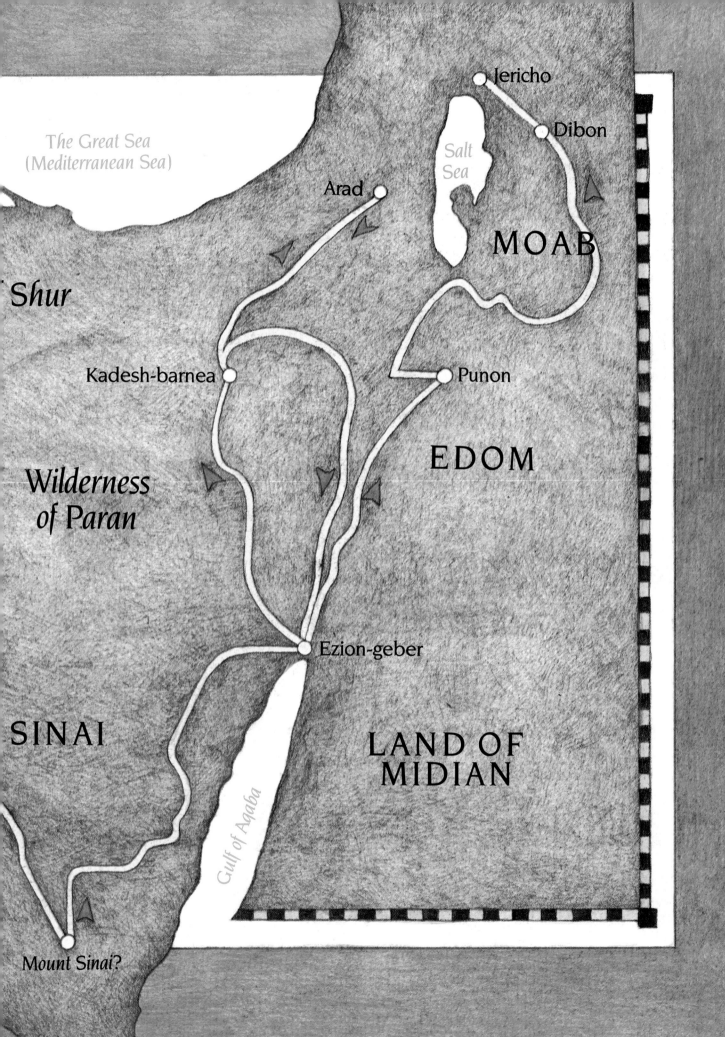

Jericho

Dibon

The Great Sea
(Mediterranean Sea)

Salt
Sea

MOAB

Shur

Arad

Kadesh-barnea

Punon

EDOM

Wilderness
of Paran

Ezion-geber

SINAI

LAND OF
MIDIAN

Gulf of Aqaba

Mount Sinai?

Above are the names and the symbols of the twelve tribes that followed Moses and Aaron out of Egypt. (It is deliberate that they have been arranged alphabetically rather than chronologically.)

For Hillel Kook and Samuel Merlin, who showed the road back.   M.C.

Thanks to Sylvia Avner and to Burt, Carole, David, Jim, Steve, Susan, Thom, Thomas and Tom for joining the trek.
                              C.M.